SCIENCE OF MIND
PRINCIPLES FOR KIDS

ABOUT
GOD
AND YOU

ABOUT THE BOOK

Most of the content in this book was created in 2012 at the request of my friend, Science of Mind minister, Rev. Doug Yagaloff. It was intended to be the first of a series of a four-book curriculum designed to introduce children to core Science of Mind concepts. Our shared vision was to create engaging material that could be used in both Sunday School and at home. This content was first published as **How to Remember Who You Are: Book 1: About God and You, Science of Mind Edition**, and features two of the Power Puppies, Sunny and Spot.

My Power Puppy characters were designed by the amazing Ken Mitchroney many years ago and were brought out of retirement to teach these important concepts. I added their heart lights.

Sadly, my friend, Doug, made his transition to Spirit in October, 2013, before our project was complete. While outlines are complete for the remaining books in the series, there is no plan to complete them at this time.

The 2016 revisions include a change in title that indicates that this book is no longer part of the series we envisioned. "Sunny" formerly appeared as "Snuggles" in the earlier edition, and the first lesson has been rewritten. All other content has remained virtually the same.

It was my privilege to know Rev. Doug Yagaloff as the embodiment of kindness and the spirit of respectful collaboration. It was his dream to share this information with Science of Mind children of all ages, and this book is dedicated to his vision.

Avianna Jones, Ph.D., 2016

Visit the website for more information and free downloadable activities

SOMforKIDS.com

For more about the Power Puppies, visit

Power-Puppies.com

ISBN-13: 978-1536877557
ISBN-10: 1536877557

MY NAME IS

_____

AND
I AM PART OF GOD!

HELLO!

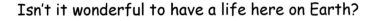

Isn't it wonderful to have a life here on Earth?

There are so many adventures for you to have. And there are so many joyful ways to feel! And it is meant to be just that way for you, always.

But sometimes, you might have questions about who you are. Or why things happen the way they do.

Lots of people ask the same questions, and they have found great answers. And the best answers always begin with remembering who you are. You are part of God, and you are never alone.

I hope this little book answers some of your questions and helps you remember how special you are and how you can live a happy, joyful life. Always.

Your friend,
Sunny

SOME BIG QUESTIONS AND ANSWERS ABOUT LIFE

CONTENTS

THE VERY BEST ME

SUNNY

SPOT

When I'm sharing and when I'm caring
I know that you can see
I'm being the me I was meant to be –
I'm being the very best me!

When I'm grateful for things I have
And share with those in need
I'm being the me I was meant to be –
I'm being the very best me!

When I'm a friend to those I meet
I know my friends can see
I'm being the me I was meant to be –
I'm being the very best me!

When I do things to help the Earth
I know the Earth can see
I'm being the me I was meant to be –
I'm being the very best me!

When my heart is full of Love
For Every Thing I see
I'm being the me I was meant to be –
I'm being the very best me!

And God is living through me
And Love is living through me
And Joy is living through me
And Peace is living through me
And Kindness is living through me

And I AM the me I was meant to be
I AM the very best me!

1. WHY ARE WE HERE?

"Hey, Sunny! Are you ready to go?" Sunny's friend, Spot, asked.

Sunny was on her way to play the best game of all – The Discovery Game on Planet Earth! It's a game where God gives you special gifts and talents to discover and guides you on great adventures. And as you play, God lives through you and grows with you. It's the best game EVER!

"Yes! Yes! Yes!" Sunny answered excitedly. "I can't wait!"

God helped Sunny create her very own game, which was perfect for her. All players' games are different, and Sunny liked that. It made her feel like the special part of God she is. Sunny smiled when she thought of how grateful she was to be chosen to play.

"It's almost time. Just a little while longer!" Spot said.

Spot knew that Sunny had to wait for the perfect time and place to begin her game, and her wait was almost over. Spot was going to play too, but not yet. Soon he would be ready to start his game and have his own adventures. He knew that he would find his way to meet Sunny so they could be good friends and play the Discovery Game together.

"Thanks, Spot! I'm ready!" Sunny said.

As she waited, Sunny thought of special God had given her. God gave Sunny the gift of Beauty to discover. Sunny knew that when she discovered Beauty in herself, she would see Beauty in all things and in all its forms, and God would see it, too.

It was easy for Sunny to feel Beauty. She saw it in Every Thing, Every Where. And as she saw Beauty, her Love for Every Thing, Every Where grew. And as the Love within her grew, she knew that God grew, too, and was living through her at that very moment.

"That's what the Discovery Game is really all about," Sunny thought.

"It's time, Sunny!" Spot announced. All Sunny's friends gathered around her. They were excited for her and knew that they would join her soon.

WE'RE HERE TO PLAY THE DISCOVERY GAME!

"Got your plan?" Sunny's friends asked.

Sunny thought about her plan from start to finish. She saw all the challenges she had planned, all the people she would meet to help her grow, and all the ways she would use her gifts. She knew she would discover all these things as she played. And she knew that God would always be with her.

"Got it!" Sunny said. She loved her plan. It was perfect for her.

"Now get ready to forget it, Sunny!" her friends laughed.

Sunny knew that playing the Discovery Game meant forgetting your plan so you could discover it again as you played. That's what makes the game so exciting!

"Your blindfold is all ready for you! And it's beautiful, Sunny!" her friends said.

Sunny knew that you can't play the Discovery Game without a blindfold. It's the thing that makes you forget your plan, so you can discover it as you play on Earth.

And at that very moment in time and space, Sunny's portal to Earth opened. She was on her way!

"Don't forget to activate your Heart Light, Sunny!" her friends shouted to her as she moved through her portal. "It will help you see through your blindfold. And keep it clear so we can talk to you!"

"And watch out for the dark Heart Clouds!" they warned.

That was the last thing Sunny heard as she continued her journey between the worlds.

And all at once she stopped and new feelings overwhelmed her. "I feel really strange," Sunny thought. And then she knew why. She was in her blindfold and her Discovery Game had started.

"I'm here! I have my blindfold on!" Sunny excitedly called to her friends through the portal.

"Happy Birthday, Sunny!" her friends cheered. "But you don't need to call it a blindfold anymore. You can call it what the other players do – It's your Earth body!"

Sunny was so happy that she had made it to Earth and into her Earth body! She celebrated with her friends. They would be playing soon and she couldn't wait to play the Discovery Game with them!

As time passed, Sunny noticed that her friends messages were getting fainter. It was harder to hear them. She knew what was happening. Her portal was beginning to close.

She felt as if her friends were getting farther away from her, and she had her first moment of fear. "Oh my goodness, the hard part of the game is starting."

Sunny felt more and more separate from her friends who were on the other side of the portal. She felt separate from Every Thing.

Sunny couldn't remember her plan, or how to reach her friends. She couldn't even feel God's love within her. Sunny was afraid.

Of course, God was still part of her, and her friends were still connected to her. She just couldn't feel them. As they watched over her they knew she was feeling what all players feel when they begin to play the Discovery Game – fear and loneliness and confusion. But they knew how to help.

"It's time to activate your Heart Light!" Sunny's friends shouted.

It was very faint, but Sunny heard her friends' message coming from the other side of the portal.

"Activate my Heart Light?" Sunny had forgotten what that meant.

But then, from deep inside her heart came a rush of Love. She knew it was God guiding her, and she knew exactly what she had to do!

Sunny remembered that the portal where God lived was inside her Earth heart now. That was her Heart Light! And she knew just how to activate it. All she had to do was to remember it was there. It was so simple!

And with just a thought of her connection with God, and with Every Thing, Every Where, Sunny's heart opened and her Heart Light began to shine brightly. And she could hear her friends again!

"Can you hear me?" Sunny called to her friends.

"Of course we can," her friends answered. "And we can't wait to get to Earth to play the Discovery Game with you!"

"Yay! My Heart Light is working," Sunny answered back.

And at that moment, another rush of God's Love flowed from Sunny's heart. She felt God, living in her heart, always loving and supporting and guiding her.

And Sunny knew she had made the best discovery ever.

I AM HAPPY TO BE ON EARTH! HERE ARE SOME GREAT THINGS I'VE DISCOVERED SO FAR ...

2. WHAT IS GOD?

Sunny was walking home from school one day, and she heard some people talking about God. She heard them say, "God is Love." That made her feel good. And then she thought about something else she heard about God. She heard someone say, "God is All There Is."

Sunny was curious. "What is God, anyway?" she thought.

 WHAT HAVE YOU HEARD ABOUT GOD?

As Sunny walked along, she saw her friend, Spot. She was so glad to see him! Spot always seemed to know the answers to everything! It was almost as if she had known him forever. And Spot always seemed to appear every time she had a question about how things work on Earth.

Sunny told Spot all the things she had heard about God, and then she asked, "What is God, anyway?"

Spot was always glad to help Sunny. "You have heard people say that 'God is Love.' And that's true. God is the Energy and Spirit of Love. But God is much, much more!" Spot said.

"God is the Energy of Love and ALL things that are Good!"

And then another question popped into Sunny's mind. "What is Energy?" she asked.

Spot knew that it wasn't easy to understand invisible things! "Energy is something real, but you can't see it with your eyes or touch it with your hands. Energy is invisible, and it's in Every Thing, Every Where."

Sunny was still curious. She didn't know that there were real things that she couldn't see or touch.

"I'll show you how to feel God," Spot said. "Think of things that feel Good."

Sunny closed her eyes and thought about Good things. She thought about having fun with her friends and laughing together. She thought about how good she felt when she had great ideas.

She thought about her family and how they loved her and hugged her. She thought about hearing the birds sing in the morning. She thought about how the breeze tickled her skin. She thought about how exciting it was to see a rainbow. And as she thought about those things, she smiled and felt happier and happier!

Spot smiled, too. "You are thinking God Thoughts!" Spot said. "God Thoughts make you feel Good when you think them. And when you feel Good, you feel God!"

Spot continued, "And your feelings are real things, even though you can't see them or touch them with your hands."

GOD IS LOVE! AND GOD IS EVERY WHERE!

Sunny understood that when she thought God Thoughts, she felt Good. And when she felt Good, she felt God!

And then Spot said, "This is the lesson of Life. When you feel Good, you know you feel God."

 WHAT OTHER GOOD THINGS CAN YOU THINK OF?
THOSE ARE GOD THOUGHTS!

"God is Light and Life and Peace and Power and Joy and Beauty and Harmony and Abundance and Creativity and all Good things!" Spot said.

Thinking God Thoughts was fun! But then, Sunny remembered something else she heard someone say. "What does it mean when people say, 'God is All There Is?'" Sunny asked.

Spot answered, "Every Thing, Every Where is made of God's Energy, so God is All There Is!"

"Every Thing, Every Where?" Sunny asked.

"Every Thing, Every Where," Spot answered. "God is Every Thing you can see, and Every Thing you can't see."

 LOOK AROUND YOU!
EVERY THING YOU SEE IS PART OF GOD!

Sunny looked around. There were trees and streets and houses and cars. "Where did all these things come from?" Sunny asked.

Spot answered, "There was a time when God was just invisible Love Energy. And then God had a Thought. It was the greatest Idea ever! God thought to create a place where Love could be seen and touched, and felt."

And then Spot said, "And that Thought mixed together with God's Love Energy, and God created the Earth and all the things on it. God created all the things you can see, like twinkling stars and singing birds and tall mountains and flowing rivers. God also created all the things you can't see, like music and warm summer breezes and the Love you feel in your heart."

Sunny looked around. It was like she was seeing things for the first time. And she had an idea. "So because Every Thing, Every Where is part of God, that's what people mean when they say, 'God Is All There Is,'" she said.

Spot nodded and smiled.

Then Sunny said, "And because God Is All There Is, then Every Thing, Every Where is connected! And I'm part of Every Thing and Every Thing is part of me."

"That's right," Spot said. "We are all connected because we are all part of God."

Sunny felt her heart grow, and she felt more Love than she had ever felt before. She felt Love for Every Thing, Every Where. And she felt like she was just remembering things that she had always known.

She realized this was God's Love and she could feel it flowing out to Every Thing, Every Where. And she knew that when she felt Love, she felt God.

Sunny was so happy. She knew for sure what God is!

I AM PART OF GOD! HERE ARE SOME OF THE WAYS GOD LIVES THROUGH ME ...

3. WHO AM I?

One day, Sunny looked in the mirror and thought, "Who am I?" She knew that she had a body, because she could see it and feel it. But she had thoughts and feelings she knew she couldn't see. "Who am I really?" she wondered.

Sunny decided to find her friend, Spot. He always helped her answer her questions! And just as she thought about him, she saw him.

"Who am I, Spot?" Sunny asked excitedly.

"Why, you're Sunny, of course!" Spot answered.

"Yes, but who am I REALLY?" Sunny asked.

"Oh, you want to know who you REALLY are!" Spot replied. "Well, that's a great question!"

"You are an amazing Being, Sunny! There are so many special things about you that are important for you to know!"

Sunny was excited! "Tell me about me, Spot!"

"Let me begin at your beginning. Once upon a time, God had a wonderful idea – God thought of YOU! And God's thought of YOU mixed with God's Love Energy and created a "Big You" that you can't see with your eyes, but you can feel with your heart. Some people call this part of you your Soul, or your Real Self, or your Perfect Self. And some people call this part of you your Inner Friend. I call this part of me my Best Friend Forever."

 WHAT DO YOU CALL YOUR "BIG YOU"?

"So I'm part of God!" Sunny said excitedly. "And there's a bigger part of me that I can't see! I get it!"

Then Sunny had another question, "Why am I here on Earth?"

"There are lots of places for you and God to play together, but God knew that you would have the greatest time playing on Earth!"

Sunny was even more excited! "So I'm part of God, and we're playing together on Earth!"

"Yes!" said Spot. "You're a special part of God having an adventure on Earth!"

Then Sunny had another question, "Where did the Earth come from?"

"God created the Earth as a place where God's Love Energy could be seen and touched and felt. But in order to play on Earth, everyone has to have an Earth body, so God created the perfect body just for you!"

"God knew that it would be fun to play in small bodies and big bodies, and as boys and girls, and in all different colors, too! And just like all the flowers in a beautiful garden are different, God made you

I'M PART OF GOD HAVING AN ADVENTURE ON EARTH!

different from everyone else. And that's what makes you so special!"

 WHAT MAKES YOUR BODY SO SPECIAL?

And then Spot said, "God knew that you would have a great time playing on Earth, and to make it the most fun for you, God gave you talents and gifts to use here on Earth that make you special."

 WHAT SPECIAL TALENTS DO YOU HAVE?

Sunny felt so good, knowing that she was such a special part of God!

"And because you and God are partners in your adventure here on Earth, it's important for you to be able to talk to your invisible Inner Friend – the part of you that is God's pure Love Energy. So God gave your body a special heart where your Inner Friend lives."

"It's nice to think of this part of you as your Best Friend Forever. Your Best Friend Forever is always Free and Happy and full of Light and Love and Good Ideas! And your Best Friend Forever already has ALL the talents and gifts God gave you and can help you discover them, enjoy them, and share them with the whole world!"

"Your Best Friend Forever is never afraid and is always looking out for you. It connects you to Every Thing, Every Where. It guides you, plans great adventures for you, and connects you to all the people, places, and things you will ever need to enjoy your life on Earth."

"Your Best Friend Forever will be your partner for your whole life. And your Best Friend Forever will live forever."

Sunny said, "So that means that I'm never alone!"

"You are NEVER alone," Spot said. "Your Best Friend Forever is always with you."

"I am so happy to have a Best Friend Forever that is always with me and wants the best for me, and loves to have great adventures!"

And then Spot said, "And God also knew that you would need a mind to have great ideas with, so God gave you a wonderful mind to think with and create with."

Sunny smiled a big smile and felt God in her heart. She was so glad that Spot helped her remember who she REALLY was – A part of God having a great adventure on Earth with a Best Friend Forever who would always be with her.

I AM MORE THAN YOU CAN SEE WITH YOUR EYES!
THIS IS ME WITH MY BFF AROUND ME ...

4. WHAT'S THE DISCOVERY GAME?

Sunny had the best day ever! It wasn't because of the fun she had at recess, or the good grade she got on her test, or how happy she felt when she got up in the morning. It wasn't because of any of those things!

She was happy because she had discovered something wonderful about herself. And she couldn't wait to tell her friend, Spot! And just then, she saw him across the street.

"Spot!" Sunny shouted. "I'm so glad to see you! I have something to tell you! I'm so excited!"

Spot always looked forward to hearing about wonderful things that happened to his friends.

"Tell me about it, Sunny!" Spot said.

Then Sunny said, "My parents gave me some paint and paper and I painted a picture of the most beautiful flower blooming outside my window!"

"That's wonderful!" Spot said. "I would love to see it. Will you share it with me?"

Sunny continued excitedly and shared her picture with Spot. "I didn't know I could paint such a pretty picture!"

 WHAT SPECIAL TALENTS HAVE YOU DISCOVERED?

Spot smiled and said, "You're having fun playing the Discovery Game!"

"What's the Discovery Game?" Sunny asked.

Spot said, "Before you came to play on Earth, God gave you special gifts and talents for you to discover about yourself during your adventure here."

Spot continued, "And your gifts and talents are like hidden treasures that you discover. That's part of the fun of playing here on Earth!"

Sunny remembered playing a treasure hunt game with her friends. There were treasures hidden all around the room and she and her friends had to find them. The game started out being so much fun.

THE DISCOVERY GAME IS A SEARCH FOR THE INVISIBLE TREASURES INSIDE US!

But there was a really hard part to the treasure hunt game. Sunny and her friends had to wear blindfolds! They couldn't see anything around them and they even bumped into each other. After awhile, they weren't even sure where they were.

Some of Sunny's friends said that there weren't any treasures to find and the game was stupid. Then when someone finally found a treasure, instead of celebrating, they fought over it. Soon everyone forgot about finding treasures, and all the fighting made them scared.

Sunny remembered that what started out to be fun turned into a game that was scary. She and her friends felt confused and afraid.

 HAVE YOU EVER PLAYED A GAME WITH A BLINDFOLD ON? HOW DID YOU FEEL?

Sunny told Spot about the game she played with her friends. "I didn't like playing that game," Sunny said. "It started out fun, but I got scared."

Spot replied, "The Discovery Game on Earth can feel that way if you don't remember who you are. But when you know that you are part of God playing the game, it can be fun and exciting!"

Spot continued, "Imagine playing that game with your blindfold on, but your Best Friend Forever was whispering to you and guiding you to where all your treasures were. There were plenty of treasures for everyone, and no one had to fight over them. And everyone was happy for you when you found your treasure."

"That game would be fun!" Sunny said.

"That's the Discovery Game!" Spot said. "You have to discover the most wonderful things about yourself. The greatest things you can discover about yourself are invisible. Like the loving feelings you have and the great ideas you have. And all the ways you feel connected to Every Thing."

"That sounds like so much fun!" Sunny said. "But how does the game end?"

"Well, Sunny, best of all, the game never ends. And your Best Friend Forever will always be there to guide you and help you find the amazing treasures inside you."

Sunny was even more excited. "I wonder what else I'll discover today!"

The two friends laughed together and looked forward to their next adventures as they played the Discovery Game.

I AM TALENTED, I HAVE GREAT IDEAS, AND I DO AWESOME THINGS! HERE ARE SOME OF THEM ...

5. WHAT ARE HEART CLOUDS?

Sunny had the worst day ever. Her best friend moved away, she forgot her homework, and people yelled at her.

As she walked home, she thought about all the things that happened, and she felt worse and worse. "I'll never have a good friend again," she thought. "I can't do anything right," she thought. "I'll never feel good again," she thought.

HAVE YOU EVER HAD A BAD DAY?
WHAT THOUGHTS WERE YOU THINKING?

As Sunny walked along, she didn't even notice that her friend, Spot, came to walk by her side.

"What's wrong?" asked Spot. "Sunny, you look so sad."

Sunny told Spot about her day. As she talked about what happened, she felt a little better. She knew that it always feels better to share with someone who cares about you.

Sunny continued, "I just can't seem to feel happy."

Spot knew right away what happened. Sunny's thoughts had made dark Heart Clouds around her heart.

"I'm so sorry all those things happened to you, Sunny. Even though all those things happened, I know you won't feel bad forever. We just have to take care of those dark Heart Clouds you created."

"Dark Heart Clouds? What are Heart Clouds?" Sunny asked.

"Heart Clouds come from the thoughts we think, Sunny. You know that when you think God Thoughts, you feel Good - and you feel God! God Thoughts are Light fluffy clouds around our hearts. But there are other thoughts we think, too. And those thoughts can make us feel sad or scared or unhappy."

Before Sunny could even ask where those thoughts came from, Spot said, "Thoughts that make us feel bad come from our imagination."

"What's our imagination?" Sunny asked.

"Our imagination is one of the most wonderful gifts God gave us. It helps us create things. And most of the time, we use our imagination to create wonderful, exciting things that haven't happened yet. But sometimes, without realizing it, we use our imagination to create things that make us feel bad." Spot said.

"So how does our imagination make us feel bad?" Sunny asked.

"Have you ever seen a scary movie? Or heard a scary story?" Spot asked. "Do you remember how you felt?"

Sunny didn't have to think very long before she remembered a story that had always scared her. "There's a movie I saw about a shark that ate people. I was so scared that I didn't even want to take a bath ever again!"

"It was your imagination that made you scared, because you believed something that wasn't real and wasn't true."

"I never thought about it that way before," Sunny said. "Beliefs are powerful things!"

"Yes, they are, Sunny! And today you used your imagination to make dark Heart Clouds around your heart. That's what made you so sad."

"And when you have lots of dark Heart Clouds, it can be hard to hear your Best Friend Forever speaking to you and giving you great ideas and guiding you."

"So how do I get rid of the dark Heart Clouds?" Sunny asked. "I don't want them around my heart!"

I WILL NEVER HAVE ANOTHER FRIEND

I WILL NEVER FEEL BETTER

I NEVER DO ANYTHING RIGHT

Spot knew the answer. "Start by looking at the thoughts in your Heart Clouds and ask yourself if they are true or not. Remember, if your thoughts feel Good, they are God Thoughts and they are True."

Sunny thought about the dark Heart Clouds that made her sad. And when she thought about them, she realized they weren't true. "I will miss my friend, but I know that I can always call her and write to her and she will still be my friend. And I know I will make new friends to play with, because I am a good friend and making friends is easy for me."

"And sometimes I make mistakes, but I'm good at solving problems and I always discover new ways to do things. So tonight I'll put my homework in my backpack so I won't forget it tomorrow." Sunny said. "And I'm already feeling better!"

"See Sunny, God Thoughts are the Truth about who you really are because you are part of God. They are made of Light and Love. And when you think God Thoughts, the dark Heart Clouds dissolve right away because they aren't true."

Sunny thought more God Thoughts, and soon she felt Love Energy flowing from her heart again. "Thanks, Spot!" she said. "I feel so much better now that I have Light Heart Clouds around my heart! I'm so happy to have a friend like you!"

I AM GOOD AT THINKING GOD THOUGHTS! HERE ARE GOD THOUGHTS DISSOLVING DARK HEART CLOUDS ...

6. HOW DO WISHES COME TRUE?

Sunny loves birthday parties! At her birthday party last week, all her friends came and they had so much fun! Her friends even sang a special birthday song to her. She had a beautiful cake with candles on it, one for every year she had been on Earth. Then the time came for her to make a wish and blow out her candles. Everyone gathered around her, waiting for her to wish for something she really wanted.

Sunny thought for a long time before she made her wish. She didn't wish for a thing, like a toy. She wished for something to happen. When she was sure about what she wanted, she was ready to blow out her candles so her wish would come true. She believed that she had to blow out all the candles at the same time, or her wish wouldn't come true, so she took the biggest big breath she could take, and blew as hard as she could!

All the candles went out except one. "Oh, no!" she thought. "Now my wish won't come true!" And with her next breath, she blew out the last candle.

 HAVE YOU EVER MADE A WISH? DID IT COME TRUE?

Sunny was disappointed as she thought about her birthday wish. Because she didn't blow out all her candles at the same time, she was afraid her wish would never come true.

And then Sunny had a great idea! "I'll ask Spot about my birthday wish! He always helps me find the answers to my questions!"

31

And just then, Spot came walking toward her.

"Spot, I'm so glad to see you!" Sunny said.

"It's always good to see you, too!" Spot said. "I had such a good time at your birthday party. Thank you so much for inviting me to share your special day with you."

Sunny told Spot how worried she was that her birthday wish wouldn't come true because she didn't blow out all her candles at the same time.

Spot smiled. "No worries, Sunny! I can tell you how wishes come true. And it doesn't have anything to do with blowing out all your birthday candles at the same time."

THOUGHTS AND FEELINGS CREATE THINGS!

"You remember that God created Every Thing, Every Where by first having a great Idea about something. And then God's Thought mixed with God's Love Energy, and when that happened, the thing God thought about came into being! And because you are part of God, you can create things, too!"

"How does that work?" Sunny asked. "Should I go get more birthday candles?"

Spot laughed. "You don't need birthday candles, Sunny. All you need is the Mind and the Heart that God gave you."

Sunny was glad she didn't need more birthday candles! She had lots of wishes!

"Let's start with your birthday wish. What did you wish for, Sunny?"

"I wished for a new friend, because my best friend moved away," Sunny said.

"That's a great wish, Sunny. Now let's get started. The first part of creating something is to remember that all things are possible. Just think about God and how God lives in your heart."

Sunny stopped and thought about God and felt God's Love in her heart. It made her so happy! She smiled a big smile.

Spot smiled, too. "Now, Sunny, think about what you want, but don't stop there. Use your imagination and feel how wonderful it will be when your wish comes true. And feel it as if it has already happened, and your new friend is part of your life. It's your imagination and your feelings together that are important."

Sunny felt good when she thought about her new friend. She imagined playing in the playground and laughing together. She felt so happy and grateful as she thought about all the good times they would have together.

"It feels so real! Like my new friend is already in my life!"

"Perfect!" Spot said. "You're creating things, just like God does, by using your imagination and your feelings together."

"Now what should I do?" Sunny asked. "My new friend feels so real, but she's not here."

"Your friend is not here YET," Spot said. "Now you have to have faith that your friend will come into your life at the perfect time. Just be ready for it to happen, and don't worry that your wish won't come true."

"Thanks, Spot!" Sunny said. "I like thinking about my new friend! It feels really good!"

Time passed, and one day Sunny saw Spot again. "Guess what?" she said to Spot. "My wish came true! I have a new friend!"

"That's great, Sunny! I'm so happy for you! I knew your wish would come true!"

"The funny thing is that it didn't happen the way I thought it would. I thought that someone new would move into my neighborhood, but it didn't happen that way. My new friend is someone I have known for a long time, we just never spent much time together before. And now we have the most fun ever!"

"That's how it works, Sunny. Your wishes are always made with your imagination and your feelings together. And sometimes you get what you wish for in ways that are even better than you can expect or imagine!"

"How does that happen?" Sunny asked.

"Remember, your Best Friend Forever plays the Discovery Game with you and knows all the wishes in your heart. And you can always count on your Best Friend Forever to guide you to wonderful things."

Sunny was ready to make more wishes, and she was so happy to know she didn't need candles to make them come true!

I AM GOOD AT MAKING WISHES COME TRUE! HERE'S ONE OF MY WISHES THAT CAME TRUE ...

7. HOW CAN I LIVE A HAPPY LIFE?

Sunny was playing with her new friend and they saw Spot. "I want you to meet Spot," Sunny said. "He is always happy, and when I'm confused or have questions about something, he always helps me find the perfect answer. And he is really nice. You will like him!"

Sunny invited Spot over and the three of them got to know each other. And then Sunny noticed something different about him. "What is that book you're carrying, Spot?"

"It's my Discovery Book. Some people might call it a gratitude journal, but it's more than that."

"What's a Discovery Book?" Sunny asked.

"It's where I write and draw pictures of things I love about my life and all the things I'm thankful for. And all the things I'm discovering about myself and the world." Spot answered.

"Would you share it with us?"

"Of course," Spot said. "I would love to share it with you."

Sunny took Spot's Discovery Book, and opened it. She looked down at a page and exclaimed, "Oh, wow! I see my name, Spot!"

"Yes, Sunny. That was the day of your birthday party. I wrote about how grateful I was to have you as my friend. And I was grateful that I could come to your party and celebrate your special day with you."

"When did you write about my party, Spot?"

"I write in my Discovery Book every night before I go to sleep. I think about all the wonderful things that happened during the day and the new things I'm grateful for, and then I write about them. And I write down all the good ideas I have, too. And tonight, I will write about how nice it was to spend time with both of you."

"And I write about all the things I discover about myself as I play the Discovery Game. This morning I discovered that I am really good at solving problems, so I'll write about that tonight, too!"

 DO YOU HAVE
A DISCOVERY BOOK?

MY DISCOVERY BOOK HELPS ME REMEMBER WHO I AM – I'M PART OF GOD!

Sunny turned the pages and saw a picture of Spot's family. "You have such a nice family," Sunny said.

"Thank you, Sunny. I am so grateful for my family. They love me so much and take such good care of me. And they help me play the Discovery Game."

Sunny turned the page again and saw a picture of Spot playing a guitar. "My family noticed that I really liked music, and they asked me if I wanted to learn to play an instrument. I really like the way a guitar sounds, so my family got me one and now I'm taking lessons. I really like it! And I discovered that I am really good at it!"

 WHAT ARE YOU
REALLY GOOD AT?

Sunny turned the page again and saw a picture of Spot playing on a team. "What's this, Spot? I didn't know you were on a team."

"I'm not on a team yet, but it's something that I want to do. It's in my imagination."

"So, you put your wishes in your Discovery Book, too?"

"Yes I do, because I know I will have the great feeling of being on a team some day. And I'm already grateful for that. And when I see pictures of my wishes, I feel excited about them happening."

"My Discovery Book helps remind me that the things I'm grateful for now first started out as my wishes. And I'm always grateful when my wishes come true."

Sunny remembered how her birthday wish came true, and how she was grateful for her new friend even before they met. "I get it! It's a great idea to be grateful for your wish coming true before it even happens!"

"That's right, Sunny. That's how wishes come true." Spot said.

 WHAT ARE SOME OF YOUR WISHES?

Sunny turned the page and saw a picture of the Earth. "Why did you draw a picture of the Earth, Spot?"

"I'm so grateful to the Earth for my body, and for the healthy food I eat and the clean water I drink. Those are gifts from the Earth that help all of us play the Discovery Game with so much joy."

WHAT DOES THE EARTH GIVE YOU
THAT YOU ARE GRATEFUL FOR?

Sunny turned to a picture of four birds in a tree. "What is this picture about, Spot?"

"That's a picture of a mama bird and a daddy bird and their two baby birds. I watched them teach their babies how to fly and find food so their babies would have good lives as grown ups. And I thought about how my parents and teachers always teach me things that will help me be free and happy when I grow up. And I am grateful for that."

 ## WHAT HAVE YOU LEARNED FROM THE ANIMALS?

"You have the greatest ideas!" Sunny said. "I love how you put them in your Discovery Book. And now I know what makes you so happy all the time."

"The thing that makes me the happiest is when I know that I'm part of God having a great life on Earth. And I know that my Best Friend Forever is always with me, helping me and guiding me as I play the Discovery Game."

"And I pay attention to how I feel, so that if my imagination makes dark Heart Clouds around my heart, I think God Thoughts right away and I feel happy again. I can always talk to God and feel God talking to me. And I use my imagination and my feelings to create wonderful things in my life."

 ## HOW DO YOU USE YOUR IMAGINATION
TO CREATE WONDERFUL THINGS?

"And when I meet someone new, I know I'm meeting God, because we're all special parts of God having our own adventures here on Earth. And I know that's how it is supposed to be!"

"People who are different than I am are playing their own Discovery Game, and I don't judge them or worry about trying to change them, because I don't know what they are here to discover. Only they know that. And if I can help them, I do, because I'm grateful for all the people who help me play my Discovery Game."

🐾 DID YOU KNOW THAT EVERYONE YOU MEET
IS PART OF GOD, JUST LIKE YOU ARE?
AND THEY ARE PLAYING THEIR OWN DISCOVERY GAME,
JUST LIKE YOU ARE.
HOW CAN YOU HELP THEM PLAY
THEIR DISCOVERY GAME?
WHO HELPS YOU PLAY YOUR DISCOVERY GAME?

Sunny was so grateful for Spot's help as she played her game. "Thank you, Spot, for all your help," Sunny said.

Spot smiled and thought about Sunny and her new friend, "And at this very moment, I am so happy being here with both of you."

Sunny and her friend gave Spot a big hug, and they all felt Love Energy flowing through their hearts, more than they ever had before.

They were so happy to be playing the Discovery Game together and so grateful for their friendship. "I'm going to write about this in my Discovery Book tonight!" they all said at the very same time.

And they all wondered what wonderful discoveries tomorrow would bring!

I AM GOOD AT CREATING A HAPPY LIFE!
HERE ARE SOME THINGS I AM GRATEFUL FOR ...

FOR GROWN UPS

How many times have we all thought, "I wish I had known about the principles of Science of Mind when I was young!" And if you're reading this, you are blessed with the opportunity to impart these powerful concepts to the children in your life.

The premise for the **Science of Mind for Kids** book is adapted from Ernest Holmes' parable of the angel. In this story, an angel comes to Earth, listens to the doom and gloom that is part of the human condition, and soon becomes worried and afraid, forgetting his angelic origin. But there is an impulse within him that guides him back to the awareness of his true identity – an angel of God.

Sunny finds herself in the same predicament as Holmes' angel – she has forgotten her true self and her unique gifts and intentions for her life on Earth. Sunny is talented and creative, but she lives in a world that can be painful and often feels sad, and she is troubled by dark Heart Clouds.

Sunny's friend, Spot, remembers who he is – a part of God having an experience on Earth – and sets a great example for Sunny. He is the teacher who magically appears when Sunny has important questions about life.

In this book you will find Holmes' familiar concepts translated for children using fresh terminology. For example, we refer to Holmes' concept of the Soul or "inner Friend" as your "Best Friend Forever."

Most of Holmes' quotations used in this program are taken from **Living the Science of Mind**. **Science of Mind Principles for Kids** may be used as the child's companion book to this important work.

ACTIVITIES

Each lesson is followed by a **Discovery Page** where kids can write about and draw pictures of something they have discovered about themselves and how things work in the world. Each prompt begins with an "I AM" affirmation to empower kids as they play the Discovery Game.

In the lesson guide to follow, there are ideas to get you started with the "I Am" Discovery Pages, and suggestions for a **group activity**.

The first lesson suggests the creation of a Discovery Book which can be the beginning of a lifelong journaling practice.

THERE'S MORE ONLINE!

FOR KIDS: There are more activities and ideas to explore.
FOR FAMILIES: There are ideas for families to explore with their children and suggestions for family activities.
FOR SUNDAY SCHOOL TEACHERS: There are suggestions for teaching the lesson and summary pages to download and print out for children to share with their families.

SOMforKIDS.com

Lesson 1

WHY ARE WE HERE?

Q: Why are we here?
A: We're here to play the Discovery Game!

In the first lesson, we meet Sunny as she gets ready to play the Discovery Game on planet Earth. It's a great game where God gives you special talents to discover and you have to find them as you play. Sunny slips through a portal into the blindfold (her Earth body) created just for her to play in, and she arrives at the perfect place and time to begin her game.

She knows that her friends will be joining her soon, but they stay behind to send her on her way. The portal between her and her friends begins to close and Sunny starts to forget who she is and why she is on Earth. Before her portal closes, her friends remind her to be sure to activate her Heart Light - the place in her heart where God lives.

Sunny activates her Heart Light and can feel God living through her. She knows that God is her Best Friend Forever and will guide her to all the wonderful adventures ahead.

FROM ERNEST HOLMES

Remembering who we really are – The Parable of the Angel (excerpts)
*A parable is told of an angel who came to visit the earth. He found himself in the usual stream of human activities and he listened to the conversations of people. For the first time he heard negative comments. Someone who was supposed to be an authority said that there might be a war and human life would be destroyed ... He began to wonder if these things might not be true, and even as he entertained the thoughts of negation to which he was listening, the brightness of his angelic presence faded into dark shadows. His form seemed to shrivel, and looking at himself he saw that he was dressed as a human being, walking the earth in fear, doubt, and uncertainty ... And yet, even in the midst of all this, something within him remembered that he was once an angel of God, living in a heaven of Beauty and a place of Peace and Joy, living in a Garden of Eden which God had provided for him. And, remembering, a determination arose within him to somehow or other find his way back to this lost paradise. This determination grew into a great hope, and as hope was renewed, a Light seemed to shine in the distance; and he seemed to have the courage to travel toward the Light. And gradually a miracle took place. As he traveled toward the Light, he found that shadows were being cast behind him, until finally he so completely entered into the Light that no shadows were cast at all, and he realized that he had been asleep, that he had had a bad dream from which he was awakening. (**Living the Science of Mind,** p.183)*

The "Discovery Game": ... *each can think of himself as playing a part in the game of life, and a good one. (**Living the Science of Mind,** p. 353)*

*... man never created himself. He merely awakes to self-discovery. (**Living the Science of Mind,** p. 112)*

*...everything that we appear to be outwardly, is always the result of some hidden fire burning at the center of our being, some Divine Reality which we did not create but which we may discover. (**Living the Science of Mind,** p. 171)*

*God is both the inventor of a game and those who play it, the author and the actor, the song and the singer. (**Creative Ideas**)*

Unique talents and gifts: *God Himself has placed a unique stamp on everyone. We should not study to be alike, but rather to develop what we really are. (**Living the Science of Mind**, p. 172)*

*There is a Divine Person back of our personality-a unique manifestation of the Living Spirit. It is never alike in any two people. This is proved by the fact that no two persons' thumb prints are alike, no two blades of grass are alike, no two anythings are identical. And yet everything is rooted in One Life, One Presence, and One Power. (**Living the Science of Mind**, pp. 171-172)*

God speaks to the heart: *God speaks to the heart through a language of feeling, a feeling which is affirmative. (**Living the Science of Mind**, p. 164)*

*God does speak to the heart more than to the intellect ... (**Living the Science of Mind**, p. 165)*

The "Best Friend Forever" – The Inner Friend (excerpts)
*You have a Friend within you who is closer than your shadow. This Friend anticipates your every desire, knows your every need, and governs your every act. This Friend is the God within your own soul, the animating Presence projecting your personality, which is a unique individualization of the Living Spirit. ... The Friend within you is continuously looking after your well-being. He always wishes you to be happy, to be well, to be radiant. Being the very fountain of your life, this Friend is a luminous Presence evermore emerging from pure Spirit, evermore expanding your consciousness. He is the High Counselor, the Eternal Guide. He is your intellect, the essence of its understanding, the nicety of its calculation, the appreciation of its temperament. There can be no greater unity than exists between you and this inner Friend. (**Living the Science of Mind**, pp. 124-125)*

*... we are guided and directed into right action; we should know that there is an Intelligence which goes before us and makes perfect, plain and immediate our way. (**Living the Science of Mind**, p. 8)*

*There is a guardian angel that accompanies everyone through life. It is the angel of God's presence in that person. It is his spiritual nature. (**Words That Heal Today**, p. 17)*
Read more online: SOMforKIDS.com

ACTIVITIES

Discovery Page: I am happy to be on Earth! Here are some great things I've discovered so far.
To get you started: Think of things you love doing, people you love being with, things that make you laugh, ways you like to play, food you like to eat, music you love to hear ...

A fun thing to do:
Make a book called, "My Discovery Book." It's a great place to hold Discovery Pages you will create as you discover new things. There is so much to discover about you and your life on Earth that you could make a new page every day! (Jump ahead to Lesson 7 to see how Spot uses his Discovery Book.)

You can buy a 3-ring binder (or be Earth-friendly and use a recycled binder) and download a cover and Discovery Pages from the website, SOMforKIDS.com.
OR
You can make your own book! You can use cardboard for the covers, punch holes to hold your paper, and bind with metal rings, twist ties, yarn, or string. You could even clip your pages together. Decorate with things you recycle from magazines and craft supplies.

WHAT IS GOD?

Q: What Is God?
A: God is Love. And God is Every Where and in Every Thing

In this lesson, Sunny is curious about what God is. Spot explains that God is the energy of Love and God is All There Is. Spot also shows Sunny how to feel God. Sunny learns about **God Thoughts** – thoughts that Feel Good when you think them. She learns that when she feels Good, she feels God. Sunny also learns about other aspects of God.

Sunny also wants to know where things come from, and Spot teaches her about how all creation takes place – first there is a thought, and the thought mixes with God's Love Energy, and something comes into being.

Sunny realizes that Every Thing, Every Where is part of God, and that God is All There Is. And she understands that she is connected to Every Thing, Every Where.

FROM ERNEST HOLMES

*God is all there is. God is Love. Love is the motivating Power of the whole Universe. God is in everything; God is in everyone. (**Living the Science of Mind,** p. 403)*

*The fact that we are dealing with invisible forces makes them no more intangible than any other force of nature with which we deal. All life is invisible, all energy is invisible, all causation is invisible. The Principle of Mind is invisible and Its practice is invisible, but Its results are the Word made flesh. (**Living the Science of Mind,** p. 289)*

*... we were born into the human kingdom from the great mother heart of Love and Life. (**Living the Science of Mind,** p. 428)*

ACTIVITIES

Discovery Page: I am part of God! Here are some ways God lives through me.
   Think about times when you feel Love toward someone or something. That's God you feel. Think about times you are kind to other people and other beings who live on the Earth, like animals and insects and trees and plants. That's God being kind to all living things.

A fun thing to do:
   Play the "I see God" game – Take a walk and look around. Every Thing you see is part of God! (And Every Thing you can't see is part of God, too!)

WHO AM I?

Q: Who Am I?
A: I'm part of God having an adventure on Earth!

Sunny is curious about who she REALLY is, and Spot explains the concept of the individualization of God which some call the Soul, the "Real You," or "the Friend within you." Spot calls this part of you your **Best Friend Forever** and helps Sunny feel her own invisible energy.

FROM ERNEST HOLMES

You have a Friend within you who is closer than your shadow. This Friend anticipates your every desire, knows your every need, and governs your every act. This Friend is the God within your own soul, the animating Presence projecting your personality, which is a unique individualization of the Living Spirit.

This Friend within you is Infinite since He is a personification of God. He is not limited by previous experiences which you may have had, by present conditions, or passing situations. He has no inherited tendencies of evil, lack, or limitation. He has never been caught in the mesh of circumstance. He is at all times radiant, free, and happy.

To your intellect this invisible Friend may seem to be someone else, not your Real Self, but such is not the case. Some have believed that this Friend within you is a mediator between you and Creative Spirit. Others have believed Him to be the reincarnation or the rebirth of your previous self, while others have sincerely believed Him to be some discarnate soul. But you are not to accept such beliefs, for the Real Person within you is a direct personification of the Universal Spirit. He is your Inner, Absolute, and Perfect Self.

The Friend within you is different from all other persons, yet He is united with all. There is some part of you which reaches into the nature of others, irresistibly drawing them to you and drawing you to them, binding all together in one complete Unity. Right now you are one with all persons, all places, all events.

The Friend within you lives in a state of poise. He is above fear, He is beyond hurt, He is sufficient unto Himself.

*The Friend within you is continuously looking after your well-being. He always wishes you to be happy, to be well, to be radiant. Being the very fountain of your life, this Friend is a luminous Presence evermore emerging from pure Spirit, evermore expanding your consciousness. He is the High Counselor, the Eternal Guide. He is your intellect, the essence of its understanding, the nicety of its calculation, the appreciation of its temperament. **Read more online**. (**Living the Science of Mind**, pp. 124-125)*

ACTIVITIES

Discovery Page: I am more that I can see with my eyes! This is me with my BFF around me.
> *Think of what Love would look like if you could draw it. It could be sparkly or wavy and be made of beautiful colors. This is your invisible BFF, who surrounds you.*

A fun thing to do:
> *Feel your invisible energy – Hold your hands apart, like there is an invisible ball between them. Move your hands around the invisible ball. You will feel your own energy and part of you that you can't see with your eyes – your BFF!*

WHAT'S THE DISCOVERY GAME?

Q: What's the Discovery Game?
A: It's a search for the invisible treasures inside us!

Sunny is excited because she is discovering more wonderful things about herself. Spot tells her that she is playing the "Discovery Game" – the model for our experience on Earth. The goal of the Discovery Game is to remember that we are God having an adventure on Earth, and to discover the gifts and talents that make us who we are. And we play the game with our Best Friend Forever who is always guiding us to new discoveries.

FROM ERNEST HOLMES

*It will help if we decide to play the game of life in a happy way. (**Living the Science of Mind,** p. 272)*

*… each can think of himself as playing a part in the game of life, and a good one. (**Living the Science of Mind,** p. 353)*

*… man never created himself. He merely awakes to self-discovery. (**Living the Science of Mind,** p. 112)*

*…everything that we appear to be outwardly, is always the result of some hidden fire burning at the center of our being, some Divine Reality which we did not create but which we may discover. (**Living the Science of Mind,** p. 171)*

*God is both the inventor of a game and those who play it, the author and the actor, the song and the singer. (**Creative Ideas**)*

ACTIVITIES

Discovery Page: I am talented I have great ideas, and I do awesome things! Here are some of them.
EVERYONE has talents and great ideas! You might be great friend to special people in your life. You might be kind to all living things. You might have solved a problem with a great idea. You might be a good artist, or game player, or athlete, or singer. You are amazing!

A fun thing to do:
Play the Discovery Game with a blindfold on. In this game, a friend will hold your hand and whisper in your ear as they guide you to your treasures. The treasures could be nice things that your friends have written about you on little pieces of paper that they hide around the room. Your friends have noticed the things you are good at, kind things you have done for them and for others, and lots of things they like about you.

After you have found your treasures, you can take a turn at being a guide for your friend. The Discovery Game is fun when you have someone you trust guiding you to your treasures!

WHAT ARE HEART CLOUDS?

Q: What are Heart Clouds?
A: Thoughts that we have that surround our hearts

Sunny had a bad day and created some dark Heart Clouds. Spot explains that dark Heart Clouds are beliefs that come from our imagination when we imagine things that aren't true about ourselves. They make it hard to hear our Best Friend Forever talking to us and guiding us, but there's always a way to get rid of them.

Spot explains that thinking God Thoughts – the Truth about us – dissolves dark Heart Clouds. Sunny dissolves her dark Heart Clouds by thinking God Thoughts, and she feels better.

FROM ERNEST HOLMES

No plainer statement of the Law of Cause and Effect could be given than this. We may wire the building for electricity, and have light. But if the wire is short-circuited something will go wrong and we shall again be entangled with darkness. The darkness was never a thing of itself; it was merely a confused state. The source of our supply was not really cut off; it stopped at our place of confusion and no longer functioned for us. This is a perfect statement of the mental Law of Cause and Effect and it again warns us that we must be aware of the use we are making of the Law; we must keep our thought straight. (Living the Science of Mind, p. 338)

Love dissolves fear. (Living the Science of Mind, p. 331)

ACTIVITIES

Discovery Page: I am good at thinking God Thoughts! Here is are God Thoughts dissolving Dark Heart Clouds.
   Think of some things that are not true that could create dark Heart Clouds. There are LOTS of them around all of us! Do not believe them! Then think of the God Thought that would dissolve the dark Heart Cloud. The more you do this, the faster you will be able to spot things that are not true about you. And you will know how to dissolve the dark Heart Clouds before they find their way into your heart space.

A fun thing to do:
   Pop dark Heart Clouds with God Thoughts. You can use soap bubbles. Think of thoughts you have that might make dark Heart Clouds. Those are things you tell yourself that aren't true about you. You don't want them around your heart! For every dark Heart Cloud, think a God Thought that is true. Then make soap bubbles and pretend they are dark Heart Clouds. Then think a God Thought and pop the bubbles!

Lesson 6

HOW DO WISHES COME TRUE?

Q: How do wishes come true?
A: Thoughts and feelings create things

At Sunny's birthday party, she couldn't blow out all the candles on her cake at the same time, and she was afraid her birthday wish wouldn't come true. Spot explains that you don't need birthday candles to create the feelings that you want. We create what we want by using our imagination and feelings together. Then we have faith that our Best Friend Forever will guide us to the feelings we want, sometimes in ways more wonderful than we can imagine.

FROM ERNEST HOLMES

*First, let us begin with the thought that we are all united with an Invisible Force which is creative, and that we are already One with a Universal Mind which can do anything. Next, let us consider that we are centers within this Mind, and that the sum total of all our thoughts is either silently attracting Good to us or repelling It from us. And third, let us know that we can change our thinking and, in so doing, cause the Law of Good to act affirmatively for us instead of negatively. (**Living the Science of Mind**, p. 18)*

*While we admire the intellect, we must realize that the intellect is not the creative factor in the Universe. Rather, it is feeling that is creative. ... The real creative power of the mind is deeper than the intellect. It passes into the realm of feeling and acceptance, yet it is the intellect or the self-conscious faculties that must speak the word in order that every obstruction may be cleared away. (**Living the Science of Mind**, p. 164)*

*Feeling, organized and directed, is creation. (**Living the Science of Mind**, p. 311)*

ACTIVITIES

Discovery Page: I am good at making wishes come true! Here is one of my wishes that came true.
Think of some wishes that you made that came true in a way you didn't expect. Remember it was a FEELING that you wanted to have, not a thing. Your BFF helps you have the feeling you want, sometimes in ways you don't expect.

A fun thing to do:
Practice making wishes – Know they are possible because we are part of God, Imagine them, feel like they are real, know that the feeling is on its way to you, and be ready for something new to happen! And feel how grateful you will be when your wish comes true!

Lesson 7

HOW CAN I LIVE A HAPPY LIFE?

Q: How can I live a happy life?
A: Remember who you are! You're part of God!

Sunny notices that Spot is always happy. Spot explains that his happiness comes from remembering who he really is – a unique part of God playing the Discovery Game on Earth with his Best Friend Forever to guide him. He shares his Discovery Book, and Sunny learns more about the things Spot is grateful for. She appreciates his feeling of connection to all things, his acceptance of things that are different, and his dreams for the future.

FROM ERNEST HOLMES

God's Will for every person is Happiness, Peace, and Joy. (***Living the Science of Mind,*** *p. 138*)

Man is put on earth to enjoy life and he is given the freedom to decide how he is to live; always there is placed before him the possibility of two things: to be, or not to be. (***Living the Science of Mind,*** *p. 358*)

No condemnation, judgment, or fear shall go from me to anyone or anything. (***Living the Science of Mind,*** *p. 275*)

There should be the combination of gratitude, expectancy, and joy. There should be an enthusiastic recognition that we are in partnership with the Divine and that God and Company cannot fail. (***Living the Science of Mind,*** *p. 344*)

If we disconnect ourselves from the past and find ourselves firmly rooted in God today, in Love, in hope, in joyful expectancy, and in grateful acknowledgment, and if we learn to harmonize with everything that transpires today, tomorrow will blossom like a new flower in our experience. (***Living the Science of Mind,*** *p. 193*)

ACTIVITIES

Discovery Page: I am good at creating a happy life! Here are some things I am grateful for ...
Being thankful for the things you have always help you feel happier! And when you think of all the things you are grateful for, you will feel happy to be you and happy to be playing the Discovery Game!

A fun thing to do:
If you haven't already made a Discovery Book, it could be a really good time to make one. And if you already have a Discovery Book, be sure to include all things you are grateful for, and all the things you wish for. As you make your wishes, be sure to write about the feelings you want to have, not the things you want to have.

As you write and draw pictures of things you discover about yourself and things you love about your life, you'll have a great time playing the Discovery Game!

JOIN OTHERS AT CENTERS FOR SPIRITUAL LIVING **CSL.ORG**

VISIT THE PUPPIES AND LEARN MORE AT **SOMforKIDS.com**